going for gold in 2012!

Introduction

Hello and welcome to the official Team GB and ParalympicsGB Fact File!

The Olympic and Paralympic Games are the greatest sporting spectacles in the world and this book shows what they are all about. All the sports are covered, explaining what the different events are, who takes part, how the rules work, who the brilliant British athletes hoping for gold will be – all backed up with lots of great stats and facts.

About 10,500 athletes from over 200 countries will compete at the Olympic Games and a further 4,000 athletes from 150 countries will attend the Paralympic Games a few weeks later.

The
Official Team GB
and ParalympicsGB

TEAM GB

ParalympicsGB

Fact File

Contents

After loads of superb performances from British Olympians and Paralympians at the last Games at Beijing 2008, hopes are high that we can do even better at London 2012.

Although the Olympic Games started in ancient Greece more than 2,500 years ago, the event stopped and wasn't restarted again until 1896. This means that London 2012 will be the 30th Olympic Games. In fact, London is the only city to have now been awarded the Games three times. The Paralympic Games started in 1960, so London 2012 will be the 14th Games for that event.

Hosting the Olympic and Paralympic Games is a massive job. A whole new Olympic Park has been built, housing several brand new stadiums. But there are also lots of sports taking place at the best venues in and around London and throughout the UK, all of which will provide a stunning stage for the sporting action.

So whatever your favourite event is and whoever your favourite Team GB or ParalympicsGB star is, this is the guide for you - enjoy!

TEAM GB and PARALYMPICSGB – The Story So Far

The record books show that Team GB are the third most successful nation in the history of the Olympic Games and that ParalympicsGB are the second best in the Paralympic Games. Here are some fab facts and figures.

Top Five Results In Olympic Sports

	GOLD	SILVER	BRONZE	TOTAL
Athletics	49	78	61	188
Rowing	24	20	10	54
Sailing	24	14	11	49
Cycling	18	24	21	63
Swimming	15	22	28	65

Top Five Results at Olympic Games

London 1908
56 gold (145 total)
Beijing 2008
19 gold (47 total)
Antwerp 1920
15 gold (43 total)
Paris 1900
15 gold (30 total)
Sydney 2000
11 gold (28 total)

Great Britain is the only nation to have won one gold medal in every Olympic Games.

Top Five Paralympic Games Results

New York & Stoke Mandeville 1984 138 gold (419 total)
Seoul 1988
63 gold (179 total)
Arnhem 1980
47 gold (99 total)
Beijing 2008
42 gold (102 total)
Sydney 2000
41 gold (131 total)

Top Five Results at Beijing 2008 Paralympic Games

Cycling 17 gold (20 total)
Swimming 11 gold (41 total)
Equestrian 5 gold (10 total)
Athletics 2 gold (17 total)
Archery 2 gold (4 total)

Olympic Record in London Games

	ATHLETES	GOLD	SILVER	BRONZE	TOTAL	RANK
1908	676	56	51	39	146	1st
1948	375	3	14	6	23	12th

Scottish star Launceston Elliot was Team GB's first-ever Olympic gold medallist, winning the one-handed lift Weightlifting crown in 1896.

Welcome to London

ParalympicsGB

City of Dreams

Thousands of fans will travel to London to watch the Olympic and Paralympic Games. The Games are the main attraction but London is a great city and there are loads of amazing things to do.

> London is the only city to have been awarded the Games three times.

Amazing Attractions

Buckingham Palace
The Queen's official home when she is in London, the palace's most famous feature is the balcony on which the Royal Family greet crowds after state occasions such as weddings.

Tower of London
Boasting nearly 1,000 years of history, The Tower is a former prison and is also home to the priceless collection of the Queen's Crown Jewels.

The London Eye
An awesome 135m-high Ferris Wheel on the South Bank of the River Thames, the London Eye offers unbelievable views over the city.

The Natural History Museum
One of the world's greatest museums, the Natural History Museum has more than 70 million items in its world-famous collection, including the popular collection of dinosaur skeletons.

Tate Modern
Home to a spectacular collection of modern art, the Tate Modern is a former power station and it's the most popular modern art gallery in the world with 4.7 million visitors per year.

London Zoo
The world's oldest scientific zoo, London Zoo is home to lions, tigers and gorillas, and was used as a location for *Harry Potter and the Philosopher's Stone*.

London by Numbers

14 The number of professional football clubs in the capital

15 Number in millions of tourists who visit the city each year

215 Length in miles of the River Thames

270 The number of stations on the London Underground network

310 Height in metres of the 72-storey Shard London Bridge building, the tallest in the city

7,825,000 The population of London

> There are more than 300 different languages spoken in London.

Getting Around

The London Underground, known as the Tube, is the oldest underground railway in the world. The first section was opened back in 1863 and today it boasts an incredible 250 miles of track, both above and below the streets of the capital, carrying an estimated three million people each day. But if you don't fancy getting the Tube, you could always hop on one of the 8,000 buses that operate in the city.

> There are 25 places around the world also called London.

Inside the Olympic Park

There is so much to see and do inside east London's stunning Olympic Park. Here's all you need to know about the home of the London 2012 Games.

EAST

Water Polo Arena

What's There? A 37m competition pool inside a wedge-shaped arena that has a roof made of recycled cushions.

What's On? As the name suggests, the world's best Water Polo teams will do battle here.

Aquatics Centre

What's There? An eye-catching indoor water sports stadium featuring an amazing wave-like roof.

What's On? You can catch Swimming, Diving, Synchronised Swimming, Paralympic Swimming and the swimming element of the Modern Pentathlon inside the Aquatics Centre.

Olympic and Paralympic Village

What's There? As well as sleeping in brand new apartments, athletes will also be able to enjoy chilling out in a number of restaurants and shops.

What's On? This is where the athletes and officials will eat, sleep and relax throughout the Games.

White Hall

What's There? The Basketball arena, which will be dismantled and possibly rebuilt somewhere in the UK after the Games.

What's On? Basketball, Handball, Wheelchair Rugby and Wheelchair Basketball will all take place inside the venue.

SOUTH

Olympic Stadium

What's There? An amazing track and field athletics venue built on an island surrounded by water and five spectacular bridges.

What's On? Fans will witness hundreds of action-packed races and field events inside the stadium, which will also host the Opening and Closing Ceremonies.

A 115m tall red steel tower called the Orbit is the artistic centrepiece of the park.

BMX Track

What's There? A 400m soil track featuring jumps, bumps and terrifying turns.
What's On? The men's and women's Olympic BMX racing – which is often one of the most thrilling sports to watch in the entire Olympic Games.

A whopping 14,000 cubic metres of soil were used to create the BMX Track.

Eton Manor

What's There? Nine tennis courts, four warm-up courts, three 50m swimming pools and practice pools for Synchronised Swimming and Water Polo.
What's On? The Wheelchair Tennis competition, plus it will also be a training facility for aquatic stars.

Velodrome

What's There? A beautiful state-of-the-art indoor cycling arena featuring a steeply-banked 250m wooden track.
What's On? All our track cyclists are expected to win plenty of Olympic and Paralympic medals inside the lightning-fast Velodrome.

The wonderful Olympic Stadium is a world-class, purpose-built sports arena.

Riverbank Arena

What's There? The main Hockey stadium and an all-weather warm-up pitch.
What's On? As well as hosting the Hockey competitions, the arena will also play host to Paralympic 5-a-side and 7-a-side Football.

Copper Box

What's There? A building covered on the outside with recycled copper that will change colour with age makes this a really interesting new venue.
What's On? The Fencing element of the Modern Pentathlon, Goalball and Handball are the three events on show here.

Main Press Centre

What's There? Two giant offices will house media staff from over 200 countries and a high street will link the two buildings.
What's On? This 24-hour centre will be buzzing throughout the Games as news of the results are beamed around the world.
Capacity There's enough room for 20,000 broadcasters, journalists and photographers.

4,000 British-grown trees and 300,000 plants are inside Olympic Park.

News reported from the Main Press Centre will reach around 4 billion people in total.

Athletics
Track and Road Events

Running for Gold

With 47 gold medals up for grabs, the largest single sport at the London 2012 Games will be Athletics. Team GB has a fine record on the track but four years ago, at Beijing 2008, our only gold medallist was Christine Ohuruogu, who triumphed in the women's 400m.

★ Star Turn

Name: Dai Greene
Date of Birth: 11 April 1986 (Felinfoel, Wales)
Event: 400m Hurdles
The Lowdown: The Commonwealth, European and World Champion would love nothing more than an Olympic gold medal to complete what has been a great two years. As a teenager he was a talented footballer. Swansea City were keen to sign him but Dai rejected the opportunity because he wanted to be an athlete instead. What a great decision that turned out to be!

Where and When
TRACK AND FIELD/COMBINED
EVENTS: Olympic Stadium
ROAD: The Mall
Friday 3 August – Sunday 12 August

Team GB star Dai Greene is actually called David!

TRACK EVENTS – How Do They Work?

Races on the track vary in length and are run over 100m, 200m, 400m, 800m, 1500m, 3000m, 5000m and 10,000m. The first runner over the finishing line is the winner. Some races have a hurdle event where athletes jump over obstacles – 100m (for women), 110m (for men), 400m and 3000m (called the Steeplechase). Relay races are run in teams, with four athletes in each team. Each athlete runs one stage of the race, called a 'leg', before passing a baton onto a teammate. Relay races are run over four legs of 100m or 400m.

ROAD EVENTS
– How Do They Work?

Athletics stars won't just compete for Olympic glory inside the main stadium. Five long distance races will be held around the streets of central London including the men's and women's Marathons (the women's race may feature Great Britain's amazing Paula Radcliffe), the 20km Race Walks and the men's 50km Race Walk. All five events will finish in front of Buckingham Palace on The Mall.

Two of the last three Olympic men's 110m Hurdles champions have come from Cuba.

★ Star Turn

Name: Mo Farah
Date of Birth: 23 March 1983 (Mogadishu, Somalia)
Events: 5000m and 10,000m
The Lowdown: Mo arrived in England at the age of eight with his family and grew up on the outskirts of London. By the time he was a teenager he was already winning national athletics titles and he is now proud to be the 5000m World Champion. When winning the title in South Korea last year he became the first Team GB star to land gold at a long-distance track event and he also grabbed silver in the 10,000m. He is expected to go for an amazing double in front of his home fans.

'This is my life, what I've dreamt of forever. No one can ever take it away. I will always be Olympic champion.'

Dame Kelly Holmes, double gold medallist

A marathon is raced over 26 miles and 385 yards.

Ones to Watch:

Hannah England – Won silver in the 1500m at last year's World Championships.
Andy Turner – A dark horse to land a 110m Hurdles medal.
Jenny Meadows – An 800m specialist, who is a real Team GB fan's favourite.

Athletics
Field and Combined Events

Jump and Throw

Eight field events for both men and women will entertain fans. These are made up of four jumping and four throwing competitions. Team GB's best gold medal hope is Phillips Idowu, who won silver at Beijing 2008.

JUMPING EVENTS – How Do They Work?

The Long Jump and Triple Jump involve a run and jump, landing in a soft sand pit. Long jumpers simply take a single big jump from a take-off mark but in the Triple Jump competitors take two big steps after the take-off point before launching themselves into the sand – called the 'hop, skip and jump'. If an athlete accidentally steps over the take-off point their effort won't be counted.

The next two jumping events are the High Jump and Pole Vault. Athletes attempt to jump as high as possible over a bar without knocking it off. They each have three attempts at each height to clear the bar, which is raised until a winner is found. In the High Jump, jumpers simply use their leg power to get over the bar. In the Pole Vault, jumpers use a long, bendy pole to propel themselves into the air.

Ones to Watch:

Goldie Sayers – Team GB's top javelin thrower came fourth at Beijing 2008 and wants to go one place better on home soil.

Chris Tomlinson and Greg Rutherford – These two long jumpers are great friends and rivals, and hope to push each other on to greatness.

★ Star Turn

Name: Phillips Idowu
Date of Birth: 30 December 1978 (Hackney, London)
Event: Triple Jump
The Lowdown: Born just a couple of miles away from the Olympic Stadium this Londoner, famous for his bright dyed hair, would be a very popular winner at the Games. The 2009 World Champion came second in last year's World Championships and at Beijing 2008, so is very much in the frame for glory.

THROWING EVENTS – How Do They Work?

The four Throwing events are the Discus, Hammer, Javelin and Shot Put. All are named after the objects athletes have to throw. The athlete who can throw their object the furthest wins. In the Discus, Hammer and Shot Put, athletes are allowed to spin their bodies before the throw to generate speed, but Javelin throwers have a run-up instead.

In 1993, Cuban high jumper Javier Sotomayor became the first person to jump 8ft high! His leap of 2.45m is still a world record.

★ Star Turn

Name: Jessica Ennis
Date of Birth: 28 January 1986 (Sheffield)
Event: Heptathlon
The Lowdown: Known as the golden girl of British Athletics, Jessica hopes to make her Olympic debut at London 2012 after missing the Beijing 2008 Games with an injury. The brilliant all-rounder won gold at the World Championships in 2009 and will be looking for a great performance in front of a passionate home crowd!

'I want to be the best I can. If that means doing 120 miles a week or 200 miles a week, I will do everything that it takes.'

Mo Farah, 5000m and 10,000m athlete

DECATHLON AND HEPTATHLON – How Do They Work?

The Decathlon and Heptathlon combine several track and field events into one competition to find out who the world's best all-rounders are. Men compete in the Decathlon, which is made up of 10 events over two tough days, while the women's Heptathlon has seven events. Each event is decided on points system. The athlete with most points overall wins.

Decathlon Day 1 – 100m, Long Jump, Shot Put, High Jump, 400m
Decathlon Day 2 – 110m Hurdles, Discus, Pole Vault, Javelin, 1500m
Heptathlon Day 1 – 100m Hurdles, High Jump, Shot Put, 200m
Heptathlon Day 2 – Long Jump, Javelin, 800m

Paralympic Athletics

Stadium Spectacular

The Paralympic Athletics events will provide some of the best action of the Games. The different events are held on track and field as well as the streets of London. Athletes are grouped according to disability, creating lots of races. ParalympicsGB claimed two gold, seven silver and eight bronze medals at Beijing 2008.

ParalympicsGB

TRACK AND ROAD EVENTS – How Do They Work?

The track races are held over distances from 100m to 5000m, all in the Olympic Stadium. Races are open to athletes in wheelchairs and those with prosthetic limbs, as well as competitors with visual impairments. The men's and women's Marathons will take place on the streets of the English capital and there are no heats involved.

Where and When
TRACK AND FIELD EVENTS: Olympic Stadium; ROAD EVENTS: The Mall
Friday 31 August – Sunday 9 September

'Every race I enter, I aim to win.'

David Weir, double gold medallist

A pair of carbon fibre legs used by some athletes can cost up to £15,000.

⭐ Star Turn

Name: Katrina Hart
Date of Birth: 17 May 1990 (Birmingham)
Events: 100m and 200m (T37 category)
The Lowdown: A gold medallist in the 100m (T37) at the 2011 World Championships in New Zealand, Katrina is a young sprinter with huge potential. She also won the 2010 Commonwealth Games title in Delhi.

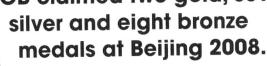

FIELD EVENTS
– How Do They Work?

One half of the field events are the throwing events. These are the Discus, Javelin, Shot Put and Club Throw. Athletes attempt to throw their object as far as possible. The Club Throw is unique to the Paralympic Games and is open to athletes in wheelchairs, who attempt to throw a wooden club the furthest distance.

The other half of the field events are the jumping events. There are three. In the High Jump, athletes attempt to jump high enough to clear a bar. In the Long Jump and Triple Jump (also known as the 'hop, skip and jump'), athletes attempt to jump as far as possible, landing in a sand pit.

Ones to Watch:
Nathan Stephens – A Javelin thrower, the Welshman narrowly missed out on the medals at Beijing 2008 but struck gold in the 2011 World Championships in New Zealand.
Stefanie Reid – A bronze medallist in the 200m (T44) at Beijing 2008, Reid is hotly tipped for gold at London 2012.

The number of British records held by David Weir, at 100m, 200m, 400m, 800m, 1500m and 5000m. 6

11.03

Time in seconds recorded by Brazilian Lucas Prado on his way to Paralympic gold in the 100m at Beijing 2008.

Visually impaired athletes run their races with a sighted partner who 'guides' them.

The number of Athletics gold medals awarded at the Beijing 2008 Paralympic Games. 160

The length in metres of Nathan Stephens' Javelin Throw in the 2011 World Championships – a new world record. 39.11

Archery

On Target
Team GB has won nine medals in Archery since first taking part in the sport at the London 1908 Games. Our most recent medallist was Alison Williamson, who won bronze at the Athens 2004 Games.

Team GB won a gold and three bronze medals when Badminton was a demonstration sport at the Munich 1972.Games

How Does It Work?
In the Individual events, archers fire a total of 72 arrows at the target, which is 70m away. The best ones then compete in best of five sets to decide the winner. More points are awarded for the closer they get to the middle of the circular target and the winner is the competitor with the highest number of points. In the Team events, each team consists of three archers, who each shoot eight arrows in a match.

Badminton

How Does It Work?
Played on a rectangular court measuring 44ft x 17ft for singles or 44ft x 20ft for doubles and using a 5ft high net, players need 21 points to win a game and a typical Badminton match is the best of three games.

Over the Net
Badminton made its full debut at the Barcelona 1992 Games but it was not until Sydney 2000, when Simon Archer and Joanne Goode won bronze in the Mixed Doubles that Team GB first tasted success.

Star Turn
Name: Nathan Robertson
Date of Birth: 30 May 1977 (Nottingham)
Event: Mixed Doubles
The Lowdown: A former World Championship and Commonwealth gold medallist, Nathan made history when he and Gail Emms claimed Team GB's first-ever silver medal in Badminton at Athens 2004.

Basketball

Where and When
White Hall and North Greenwich Arena, Saturday 28 July – Sunday 12 August

Luol Deng is Britain's biggest star and currently plays in the NBA in America for the Chicago Bulls.

Hoop Dreams

Basketball has been an Olympic sport for men since 1936 and for women since 1976, but Team GB are still looking for their first big success. The good news is both the men and women will be in action on home soil for London 2012.

How Does It Work?

Played between two teams of five players, the aim of the game is to shoot the ball through a hoop, which is 10ft above the ground. Two points are scored for every successful shot 'inside the area' while it is three points for an accurate, long-range shot.

Boxing

In the Ring

Team GB first sent boxers to compete at London 1908, where they won an amazing five gold, four silver and five bronze medals. Team GB has now won 14 gold medals, most recently in 2008, when James DeGale won the Middle Weight title.

Star Turn

Name: Luke Campbell
Date of Birth: 27 September 1987 (Hull)
Event: Bantam Weight (up to 56kg)
The Lowdown: A gold medallist at the 2008 European Amateur Boxing Championships, Luke is one of Team GB's brightest medal hopes for London 2012 – his first Olympic Games.

Where and When
ExCeL, Saturday 28 July – Sunday 12 August

How Does It Work?

Unlike professional boxers, Olympic boxers wear protective head guards. Men fight over three rounds of three minutes each, women over four rounds of two minutes each. Points are awarded by a panel of judges for successful punches and the winner is either decided by points or if one of the fighters is hurt and has to stop.

Canoeing

Paddle Power

Canoeing became an Olympic sport in 1936 but Team GB had to wait until 1992 for its first medal. At the last three Games, Britain has won nine medals, including a first-ever gold when Tim Brabants won the Men's K1 1000m event at Beijing 2008.

How Does It Work?

Canoeing has two events – Sprint and Slalom. The Sprint events are head-to-head races held on a lake while in the Slalom events, racers have to complete a zig-zag course on white water rapids against the clock. There are two different types of boat in the sport – canoes and kayaks – both of which have their own Sprint and Slalom events.

Where and When
SLALOM: Lee Valley White Water Centre, Sunday 29 July – Thursday 2 August
SPRINT: Eton Dorney, Monday 6 – Saturday 11 August

★ Star Turn

Name: Rachel Cawthorn
Date of Birth: 3 November 1988 (Guildford)
Event: Sprint Kayak
The Lowdown: Rachel competes in the Sprint Kayak Single events and hit the headlines in 2010 when she claimed a bronze in K-1 500m race at the World Championships in Poland – the first British women ever to win a Canoeing medal at the championships.

Equestrian

Saddle Up

Britain's riders and horses have been competing in the Olympic Equestrian events since 1912 and so far they have won 27 medals, including six golds.

More than 200 horses from 41 nations were in action at the Beijing 2008 Games.

Where and When
EVENTING: Greenwich Park, Saturday 28 July – Tuesday 31 July
DRESSAGE: Greenwich Park, Thursday 2 August – Thursday 9 August
JUMPING: Greenwich Park, Saturday 4 – Wednesday 8 August

How Does It Work?

There are three disciplines – Dressage, Jumping and Eventing. All three have Individual and Team events. Dressage is a test of horse and rider's coordination and control, while Jumping involves clearing a series of fences in an arena. Eventing is dressage and jumping with a cross country test as well.

Fencing

Sword Play

An event at every Olympic Games, Team GB won its first Fencing medals at London 1908 with a silver in the Team Epée competition. We have not won a medal in the last 11 attempts but did claim a famous gold in Australia in 1956, when Gillian Sheen was triumphant in the women's Individual Foil.

How Does It Work?

There are three different types of sword in Olympic Fencing – Foil, Epée and Sabre. Competitors score points by 'hitting' their opponents with their weapons and the competitor with the most points wins. Electronic scoring is used to tell whether or not a point has been scored. Fencers wear special gear that stops their opponent's sword hurting them, including a unique face mask and body armour.

The traditional colour for a fencer's uniform is white but coaches wear all black.

Where and When
ExCeL, Saturday 28 July – Sunday 5 August

★ Star Turn
Name: Richard Kruse
Date of Birth: 30 July 1983 (London)
Event: Foil
The Lowdown: Richard has already competed at two Games, reaching the quarter-finals in the Individual Foil at Athens 2004. He also won a silver medal at the 2009 European Championships in Bulgaria.

Handball

Where and When
Copper Box and White Hall, Saturday 28 July – Sunday 12 August

Fast Fun

An Olympic sport since its indoor debut at the Munich 1972 Games, Handball is hugely popular in Europe but has yet to make a big impact in the UK. Team GB's men's and women's Handball teams will be making their Olympic debuts in 2012.

How Does It Work?

A fast and physical sport, Handball features two teams of seven players each aiming to throw a leather ball into their opponent's goal. The team with the most goals after two periods of 30 minutes is the winner. The sport is usually played indoors on a court measuring 130ft x 66ft, with a goal in the centre of each end.

21

TEAM GB and PARALYMPICSGB
Trivia Quiz

How much do you know about the mighty Team GB? Test yourself in our tricky 10 question quiz and see if you can earn maximum points...

1. Which two Team GB athletes won gold at last year's World Athletics Championships in Daegu?
a) Phillips Idowu and Mo Farah
b) Dai Greene and Mo Farah
c) Jessica Ennis and Mo Farah

2. What's the real name of the Team GB Equestrian legend?
a) William Fox-Pitt
b) Jason Fox-Pitt
c) Frankie Fox-Pitt

3. Where was Team GB Tennis star Andy Murray born?
a) Liverpool
b) Glasgow
c) Birmingham

4. What position did Team GB finish in the medals table at the Beijing 2008 Games?
a) 1st
b) 4th
c) 8th

5. What Football team does Mo Farah support?
a) Manchester City
b) Tottenham Hotspur
c) Arsenal

6. Which Paralympic Swimming sensation won two gold medals in Beijing 2008 at the age of just 13?
a) David Roberts
b) Heather Frederiksen
c) Ellie Simmonds

7. Which brothers compete for Team GB in the Triathlon?
a) Jonathan & Alistair Redgrave
b) Jonathan & Alistair Greening
c) Jonathan & Alistair Brownlee

8. Which ParalympicsGB athlete is considered to be the best all-round wheelchair racer on the planet?
a) David Weir
b) David Wallace
c) David Winterbottom

Wordsearch

9. Which sport is Victoria Pendleton a leading gold medal hope for Team GB?
a) Cycling
b) Archery
c) Gymnastics

1. Venue for the Beach Volleyball. _____ Parade (11)
2. The main attraction at Madame Tussauds (8)
3. A tasty vegetable and famous building in the city of London (7)
4. This will be the _____ time London has hosted the Olympic Games (5)
5. Nickname for London's Underground (4)
6. Wimbledon's most famous tennis court (6)
7. South London park and home to the Equestrian events (9)
8. London park that will host the Triathlon (4)
9. GB's full name (5,7)
10. Colour of a London bus (3)
11. Field event and name of London's high-speed Olympic train (7)
12. Boris Johnson is the London _____(5)
13. Home to the Crown Jewels. The _____ of London (5)
14. London's busiest airport (8)
15. Combative Olympic sport held at the ExCel (9)
16. Big wheel used to show tourists great views of London (3)
17. Wembley Stadium has a huge _____ (4)

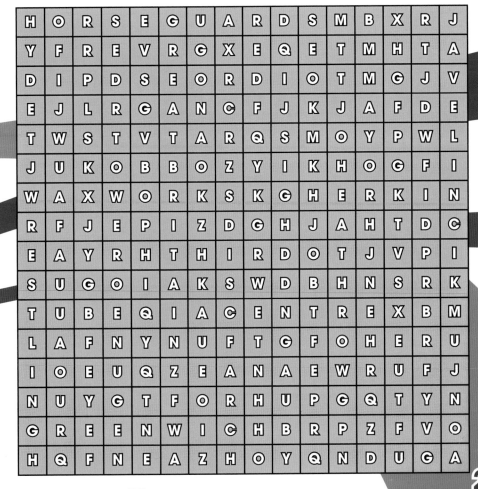

H	O	R	S	E	G	U	A	R	D	S	M	B	X	R	J
Y	F	R	E	V	R	G	X	E	Q	E	T	M	H	T	A
D	I	P	D	S	E	O	R	D	I	O	T	M	G	J	V
E	J	L	R	G	A	N	C	F	J	K	J	A	F	D	E
T	W	S	T	V	A	R	Q	S	M	O	Y	P	W	L
J	U	K	O	B	B	O	Z	Y	I	K	H	O	G	F	I
W	A	X	W	O	R	K	S	K	G	H	E	R	K	I	N
R	F	J	E	P	I	Z	D	G	H	J	A	H	T	D	C
E	A	Y	R	H	T	H	I	R	D	O	T	J	V	P	I
S	U	G	O	I	A	K	S	W	D	B	H	N	S	R	K
T	U	B	E	Q	I	A	C	E	N	T	R	E	X	B	M
L	A	F	N	Y	N	U	F	T	G	F	O	H	E	R	U
I	O	E	U	Q	Z	E	A	N	A	E	W	R	U	F	J
N	U	Y	G	T	F	O	R	H	U	P	G	Q	T	Y	N
G	R	E	E	N	W	I	C	H	B	R	P	Z	F	V	O
H	Q	F	N	E	A	Z	H	O	Y	Q	N	D	U	G	A

Answers on page 63!

Paralympic Archery

Arrow Artists

The Beijing 2008 Paralympic Games were brilliant for ParalympicsGB – their four Archery medals left them second only to hosts China. John Stubbs and Danielle Brown took gold, while John Cavanagh won silver and Mel Clarke bronze.

ParalympicsGB

How Does It Work?

Paralympic Archery uses the same rules as the Olympic Games version – archers fire 72 arrows at the target, which is 70m away. More points are awarded for the closer they get to the middle of the target. But Paralympic archers compete both standing and from wheelchairs and the Team events are open to both men and women.

Where and When
The Royal Artillery Barracks,
Thursday 30 August –
Wednesday 5 September

Boccia

Bowled Over

Boccia has been part of the Paralympic Games since 1984 and more than 50 countries across the world now play the game. ParalympicsGB won two medals in Boccia events at Beijing 2008, including gold in the Mixed Team BC1-2 competition.

How Does It Work?

The aim of the game is to throw red and blue coloured balls at a white target ball (the 'jack'). Points are awarded for balls that land closest to the target ball.

Where and When
ExCeL, Sunday 2 September –
Saturday 8 September

Star Turn

Name: Nigel Murray
Date of Birth: 22 May 1964 (Leamington Spa)
The Lowdown: A three-time Paralympic Games medallist, Nigel was a gold medallist in the Individual – BC2 class at Sydney 2000, a gold medallist in the Mixed Team BC1-2 category at Beijing 2008 and a silver medallist in the Individual – BC2 category, also at Beijing 2008. He has also been British Boccia champion an amazing seven times.

Paralympic Equestrian

Where and When
Greenwich Park, Thursday 30 August – Tuesday 4 September

How Does It Work?

Paralympic Equestrian riders compete in Dressage, which is a skilled test of coordination between horse and rider – all movements must appear as effortless as possible. There are three 'tests': a Team Test (with three to four riders per team), an Individual Championship Test and a Freestyle test.

Horses and Heroes

The Beijing 2008 Games were a fairytale for ParalympicsGB's riders, who finished top of the medals table with five gold and five silver medals. Anne Dunham and Sophie Christiansen both won Individual and Team gold, while Lee Pearson won an amazing three golds.

Star Turn

Name: Lee Pearson

Date of Birth: 4 February 1974 (Staffordshire)

The Lowdown: Already a legend, Lee has won nine Paralympic Games gold medals so far and has also claimed six World Championship and three European titles. He has won gold in each of the three events at three Paralympic Games in a row, making nine golds in total. The names of his three events are: Championship Test: Individual; Freestyle Test: Individual and Team Open. He has competed at Sydney 2000, Athens 2004 and Beijing 2008.

As well as winning two gold medals each, Anne Dunham and Sophie Christiansen both won silver medals at Beijing 2008.

Goalball

Where and When
Copper Box, Thursday 30 August – Friday 7 September

Glorious Goalball

A relative newcomer to the Paralympic Games after its debut at Toronto 1976, ParalympicsGB's last appearance in the event was in 2000 during the Sydney Games in Australia.

How Does It Work?

Designed for blind and visually impaired athletes, Goalball features two teams of three players trying to throw a ball into their opponent's goal. The ball has a bell inside to help players judge its speed and direction. A game is two halves of 12 minutes each.

25

Football

The Beautiful Game

The world's most popular sport, Football will be one of the major events at the Games as 16 men's and 12 women's teams compete for glory. Football became an Olympic sport in 1900 and Team GB won it then and again in 1908 and 1912. But the last time Team GB competed was at Rome 1960.

Football is played by over 250 million players in over 200 countries. A total of 504 men and women will play at London 2012.

The men's Football tournament in 2012 is an under-23 competition – but each side will be allowed three over-age players.

How Does It Work?

Played on a rectangular field with two teams of 11 players, the aim of football is simple – to kick or head the ball into the opposition goal. The pitch must be 90–120m long and 45–90m wide. A game is made up of two halves of 45 minutes each. Olympic rules mean England, Northern Ireland, Wales and Scotland, who usually have their own teams, will play as a combined Great Britain team.

Where and When
City of Coventry Stadium (Coventry); Hampden Park (Glasgow); Millennium Stadium (Cardiff); Old Trafford (Manchester); St James' Park (Newcastle); Wembley Stadium (London), Wednesday 25 July – Saturday 11 August

Around 2,400 footballs are expected to be used during the London 2012 competition.

Star Turn
Name: Gareth Bale
Date Of Birth: 16 July 1989 (Cardiff)
The Lowdown: Gareth started his professional career at Southampton in 2006 when he was only 16! He was snapped up by Tottenham Hotspur in 2007, where he still plays. He is one of the fastest and most exciting players in the Premier League and regularly scores from his position in left-midfield. He'll be hoping to shine just as brightly in the Team GB squad at his first Olympic Games.

Football 5-a-side

Five Alive!

5-a-side Football will be making a third appearance at London 2012 after its debut at Athens 2004. Brazil have claimed all the gold medals so far, while Great Britain qualified for the competition for the first time at Beijing 2008.

ParalympicsGB

How Does It Work?

Adapted for players with problems with their sight, the game is played on a pitch with boards all around the sides, so there are no throw-ins or corners. All players must wear a blindfold and the ball contains a rattle to help players tell where it is. A match is played in two halves, each lasting 25 minutes.

Where and When
Riverbank Arena, Friday 31 August – Saturday 8 September

⭐ Star Turn

Name: David Clarke
Date of Birth: 9 November 1970 (Harpenden)
The Lowdown: The biggest star in his native England team, David is a legend and has scored more than 100 goals for his country, as well as winning the European Championship Golden Boot award three times. The ParalympicsGB team were fifth at Beijing 2008.

Football 7-a-side

Where and When
Riverbank Arena, Saturday 1 September – Sunday 9 September

How Does It Work?

Matches are split into two halves of 30 minutes and each team must feature a mixture of players of differing physical ability. Eight men's teams will take part at London 2012.

Seventh Heaven

7-a-side Football is only for players with cerebral palsy. It has been a Paralympic sport since the New York and Stoke Mandeville 1984 Games, where ParalympicsGB claimed bronze – their best result so far.

There is no offside rule in 7-a-side Football.

Gymnastics

Head Over Heels

Gymnastics was part of the first Olympic Games in 1896 and it remains one of the most popular events of all. In fact, there are three Gymnastics disciplines – Artistic, Rhythmic and Trampoline. Team GB will be looking to add to the bronze medal Louis Smith won at the Beijing 2008 Games.

Competitors in the Trampoline Gymnastics can jump up to 10m high during a competition.

How Does It Work?

In Artistic Gymnastics, men compete on the Floor, Pommel Horse, Rings, Vault, Parallel Bars and Horizontal Bar, while women compete on the Vault, Uneven Bars, Balance Beam and Floor.

In Rhythmic Gymnastics (a combination of Gymnastics and Dance), women perform routines to music using hand props such as ribbons. On the Trampoline, men and women perform routines containing twists, bounces and somersaults. All scores are decided by judges.

Where and When
ARITISTIC: North Greenwich Arena, Saturday 28 July – Tuesday 7 August
RHYTHMIC: Wembley Arena, Thursday 9 – Sunday 12 August
TRAMPOLINE: North Greenwich Arena, Friday 3 – Saturday 4 August

Only men were allowed to compete for the first 32 years of Olympic Gymnastics. But at Amsterdam 1928, women began competing in Artistic Gymnastic events.

Soviet gymnast Larisa Latynina has won 18 Olympic medals – the most ever by an athlete.

The word 'Gymnastics' comes from the Greek for 'naked' because ancient gymnasts used to perform without any clothes!

★ Star Turn

Name: Beth Tweddle
Date of Birth: 1 April 1985 (Johannesburg, South Africa)
Event: Artistic Gymnastics
The Lowdown: Regarded as the greatest-ever British gymnast, Beth just missed out on the bronze medal on the Uneven Bars at Beijing 2008, finishing fourth. But she has won gold three times at the World Championships, in 2006 on the Uneven Bars, in 2009 on the Floor and 2010 on the Uneven Bars again.

Hockey

Hotshots

A fast-paced and hugely entertaining game, hockey has been an Olympic sport since London 1908. Great Britain's men won that first competition but their last success came at Seoul 1988, when the team defeated Germany 3-1 to claim the gold medal. Women did not compete until Moscow 1980 and Britain's ladies had to wait until Barcelona 1992 to get a taste of success for the first time, winning the bronze medal.

How Does It Work?

Contested by teams of 11 on an outdoor pitch measuring 91.4 x 55m, players use hook-shaped sticks to hit a ball into their opponents' goal. Matches are played over two halves of 35 minutes each, with five substitutes allowed per team.

Hockey gets its name from the French word *hocquet*, which means 'shepherd's crook'.

★ Star Turn

Name: Helen Richardson
Date of Birth: 23 September 1981 (Hertfordshire)
The Lowdown: One of the stars of Team GB's women's team, Helen was part of the side that won silver at the 2002 Commonwealth Games and was named Great Britain Hockey's BOA Athlete of the Year for 2010. She has played over 130 times for England and the 2012 Games will be her third.

Where and When
Riverbank Arena, Sunday 29 July – Saturday 11 August

Olympic Hockey is played on artificial turf rather than natural grass. The first time this happened was at the Montreal 1976 Games.

TEAM GB Legends

Athletes representing Team GB have won an incredible 714 medals at the Olympic Games since taking part in the first-ever competition, way back at Athens 1896. Here are six of the greatest stars to pull on the famous red, white and blue vest.

Mary Rand (Athletics)

At the age of 24, Mary became the first female Team GB star to win an Olympic track and field gold medal when she smashed the world Long Jump record at the 1964 Tokyo Games. Instead of going home, the brilliant all-rounder then went on to win a silver medal in the Pentathlon and a bronze in the 4 x 100m Relay.

Mary's record 6.76m long jump in Tokyo was extra special as it took place on a soaking wet track and against a strong wind.

Seb Coe (Athletics)

Seb landed gold medals in the 1500m at both the 1980 and 1984 Olympic Games, while also winning silver in the 800m at those events. His personal best 800m time of 1min 41.73 secs recorded in 1981 was a world record for 16 years and still remains the British record. In recent years, he has been busy as Chairman of the Organising Committee of the London 2012 Games.

Seb is a real-life Baron. His full title is Baron Coe of Ranmore.

Daley Thompson (Athletics)

The Londoner won gold medals in the Decathlon at the 1980 and 1984 Olympic Games and broke the world record four times during his amazing career. He won every major event he entered from 1979 until losing out at the 1987 World Championships. Daley was that era's Athletics king.

Daley famously whistled the British national anthem when he stood on the podium at the Los Angeles 1984 Games.

Kelly Holmes (Athletics)

Inspired by Seb Coe to take up running, Kelly was Team GB's heroine at the Athens 2004 Games, winning a gold medal double in the 800m and 1500m. More than 40,000 fans lined the streets of her home town of Hildenborough in Kent when she arrived home in an open-top bus and she went on to win the BBC Sports Personality of the Year.

Kelly used to be a Sergeant in the British Army.

Steve Redgrave (Rowing)

Team GB's most successful Olympian of all-time won gold medals at five Games in a row between 1984 and 2000 – and that's an achievement only three other athletes have matched since Athens 1896! He also won an incredible nine World Championships during his rowing career.

Steve won his fifth and final gold at the Sydney 2000 Games while suffering from diabetes.

Matthew Pinsent (Rowing)

Second only to his former rowing partner Steve Redgrave, Team GB legend Matthew won four gold medals in a row between 1992 and 2004. His lung capacity was awesome and he was once recorded as having the largest of any sportsman in the world. No wonder he didn't get tired out!

Matthew went to school at the famous Eton College and later won the Boat Race as part of the Oxford University crew.

31

Track Cycling

On Track

Great Britain's cyclists seemed almost unbeatable on the track at Beijing 2008, winning a magnificent seven gold, three silver and two bronze medals to make Team GB by far the most successful nation in the Velodrome.

How Does It Work?

There are 10 Olympic Track Cycling events – five for the men and five for women. The Sprint consists of a series of three-lap races, with riders racing head-to-head. The Keirin features up to seven riders sprinting for victory after following a motorcycle that paces the riders at the beginning of the race. There will also be two team events – the Team Sprint and the Team Pursuit. Finally, there's the Omnium, which will be making its debut at London 2012 and features individual riders competing against each other in six different disciplines.

Ones to Watch:

Bradley Wiggins – Bradley was a double Olympic champion at Beijing 2008 in the Team Pursuit and Individual Pursuit. He is now a world-class road racer.
Victoria Pendleton – Victoria claimed gold in the Individual Sprint event at Beijing 2008.

Where and When
Velodrome, Thursday 2 – Tuesday 7 August

★ Star Turn

Name: Chris Hoy
Date of Birth: 23 March 1976 (Edinburgh)
Events: Keirin, Sprint and Team Sprint
The Lowdown: Chris became the first British athlete for 100 years to win three gold medals at a single Olympic Games when he claimed a magnificent hat-trick at Beijing 2008. He now has an amazing 16 Olympic, World Championship and Commonwealth Games gold medals in his collection.

Track bikes don't have brakes – the riders slow down by putting pressure on the pedals.

Until Montreal 1976, Olympic Track Cycling events were staged outdoors.

Road Cycling

> **Where and When**
> ROAD RACE: The Mall; TIME TRIAL: Hampton Court Palace, Saturday 28 July – Wednesday 1 August

Road Racers

There are just four races in the Olympic Road Cycling programme but Team GB still came home from Beijing 2008 with a glittering gold and a superb silver.

How Does It Work?

There will be two Road Cycling events for both men and women at London 2012. In the first, the Road Race, all competitors start together and the race is 250km for men and 140km for women. The first rider to finish is the champion. The second race is the Time Trial, which is 44km for men and 29km for women. Each rider starts 90 seconds after the one in front and the winner is the rider with the fastest time.

> The Road Race has been an Olympic event right from the first Olympic Games, at Athens 1896. Only six riders took part.

> A total of 212 riders will be in action on the roads at London 2012.

★ Star Turn

Name: Mark Cavendish
Date of Birth: 21 May 1985 (Isle of Man)
The Lowdown: One of the fastest sprinters in track cycling, Mark is now the most successful British rider in the history of the Tour de France and won the 2011 World Championship Road Race in Copenhagen.

Ones to Watch:

Nicole Cooke – Already a World and Commonwealth Road Race champion, Nicole won gold at Beijing 2008.
Emma Pooley – Keep your eyes on Emma! She won silver in the Time Trial at Beijing 2008 and was the 2010 World Time Trial Champion.

33

Paralympic Cycling

ParalympicsGB

Two-Wheel Wonders

ParalympicsGB's cyclists won a sensational 20 medals at Beijing 2008, putting them at the top of the table in this event. British cyclists won an amazing five golds in Road Cycling and 12 golds in Track Cycling.

Ones to Watch:

Jody Cundy – A former Paralympic Swimming champion, Jody switched to cycling and won gold in the Kilo (1km) and Team Sprint events at Beijing 2008.
Aileen McGlyn – Aileen broke her first world record in 2004 and after winning gold in the Kilo (1km) event at Athens 2004, she won again at Beijing 2008.

How Does It Work?

Paralympic Cycling is split into two events – Road and Track. There are 32 gold medals up for grabs on the Road and 18 on the Track. The Road event is split up into the Road Race, where the riders race head-to-head, and the Time Trial, where riders compete one at a time against the clock.

The Track events are held in the Velodrome and there are Individual and Team events ranging from short sprints to long-distance races.

At London 2012, riders are grouped into classes depending on disability. There are 12 cycling classes overall, using four different types of bike – bicycle, tandem, handcycle and tricycle.

The colour of a Road cyclist's helmet reflects which class they compete in.

⭐ Star Turn

Name: Sarah Storey
Date of Birth: 26 October 1977 (Manchester)
Events: Time Trial and Pursuit
The Lowdown: A former Paralympic Swimming champion, Sarah switched to Paralympic Cycling in 2005. She made a huge impact straight away, winning two gold medals at Beijing 2008. She also made history in 2010 when she competed against non-disabled cyclists at the Commonwealth Games.

Types of Bike

There are four different types of bike:

The tandem, which is for athletes with a visual impairment. The athlete sits on the back and a sighted rider, called a Pilot, steers at the front.

The handcycle, which has pedals operated by hand. It has two wheels at the back and one at the front.

The tricycle, which is normally used by athletes whose balance would make them unable to race on a two-wheeled bicycle.

The standard bicycle, is used by all other athletes, although they are often modified.

Where and When
ROAD CYCLING: Brands Hatch, Wednesday 5 September – Saturday 8 September

TRACK CYCLING: Velodrome, Thursday 30 August – Sunday 2 September

44 The number of Paralympic Road and Paralympic Track Cycling events at Beijing 2008. There will be 50 at London 2012.

188 The number of riders who competed at Beijing 2008.

'I remember watching the Olympics when I was six ... I just wanted to pull on a GB tracksuit as soon as possible.'

Sarah Storey, double gold medallist

A total of 155 male riders and 70 women will be battling it out for the medals at London.

Riders compete using the same rules and conditions as their non-disabled counterparts at the Olympic Games.

4,000 Distance in metres of the longest track cycling race at London 2012.

BMX

Where and When
BMX Track, Wednesday 8 – Friday 10 August

Dirt Track Thrills

One of the Games' newest sports, BMX will be making only its second Olympic appearance at London 2012.

Star Turn

Name: Shanaze Reade

Date of Birth: 23 September 1988 (Crewe)

The Lowdown: A three-time winner of the BMX World Championship, Shanaze is also a double gold medallist in Track cycling and should do well at London 2012.

How Does It Work?

Riders start on an 8m-high ramp and swoop down onto a course that is full of jumps, bumps and tightly banked corners. To start with, racers are seeded by riding one at a time against the clock. This makes sure that the fastest riders don't meet and knock each other out before the final. Riders then race head-to-head in a knockout format to decide the winner.

Mountain Biking

Riders are allowed to carry a tool kit with them during the race in case anything goes wrong.

Mountain Mayhem

Mountain Biking became an Olympic sport when it made its debut at the Atlanta 1996 Games. 80 riders will compete at London 2012 in two races, one for men and one for women.

Where and When
Hadleigh Farm, Saturday 11 – Sunday 12 August

How Does It Work?

An Olympic Mountain Bike race is a very simple format. All riders start together and must complete a set number of laps of a hilly off-road course. Races last around 1hr 45min for both men and women. There are no heats and the first rider to cross the finish line wins gold.

Judo

The Art of Self Defence

Not for the faint-hearted, Judo is one of the Olympic Games' toughest and most bruising sports. Nearly 400 competitors will be at London 2012, hoping to win one of the 14 gold medals up for grabs.

How Does It Work?

An Olympic Judo contest lasts five minutes. Scores are awarded for different throws and holds but a fight is immediately stopped if a competitor is awarded *ippon*, which is the maximum score. There will be seven events for men and seven for women, all on a knockout basis.

Where and When
ExCeL, Saturday 28 July – Friday 3 August

Star Turn

Name: Mhairi Spence
Date of Birth: 31 August 1985 (Inverness)
The Lowdown: Mhairi keeps getting better and after helping Team GB to Modern Pentathlon victory at the 2009 European Championships in Germany, she won bronze at the 2010 World Cup in the UK and silver at the 2011 World Cup. London 2012 will be her first Games.

Modern Pentathlon

Multi-taskers

An exciting event, Modern Pentathlon is only for the most talented and versatile athletes. Team GB has won six medals over the years, the most recent being Heather Fell's silver in the women's event at Beijing 2008.

The 2012 Games will be the first to see the combined event (running and shooting). Previously, these were separate events.

How Does It Work?

The Modern Pentathlon takes place over a single day and has five parts – fencing, swimming, riding and the combined event (running and shooting). Fencing comes first, then competitors enter a 200m freestyle swim. Next it's riding, which takes place over a 12-jump course, then running, using a series of 1,000m runs with a shoot between each run.

Where and When
Copper Box (Fencing); Aquatics Centre (Swimming); Greenwich Park (Riding, Combined Run/Shoot), Saturday 11 – Sunday 12 August

Venues Around London

Spectacular sporting action can be found right across the capital city. Here's our lowdown on the places to be.

Earls Court

What's There? Ever since 1937, this famous west London indoor venue has been a popular exhibition centre and live music arena.

What's On? During the Olympic Games, Earls Court will be transformed into the home of Volleyball.

ExCeL

What's There? This vast exhibition centre will be split into four separate indoor venues during the Games.

What's On? Boxing, Fencing, Judo, Table Tennis, Taekwondo, Weightlifting, Wrestling, Boccia, Paralympic Table Tennis, Paralympic Judo, Powerlifting, Sitting Volleyball and Wheelchair Fencing make this one of the ultimate venues.

Greenwich Park

What's There? This historic south-east London park is a World Heritage site that's home to the Royal Observatory, the Old Royal Naval College and the National Maritime Museum.

What's On? Horse lovers will be royally entertained by the Olympic and Paralympic Equestrian events and part of the Modern Pentathlon.

> Over five million visitors from more than 200 different countries have visited London's ExCeL since the year 2000.

Hampton Court Palace

What's There? This Royal Palace was once home to King Henry VIII and is now one of London's most popular tourist attractions.

What's On? The start and finish lines of the Cycling Road Race Time Trial will be inside the Palace grounds and it's free to go and watch.

> Hyde Park's 625 acres make it bigger than the whole of the French Principality of Monaco.

Horseguards Parade

What's There? This large central London military parade ground is famous for hosting the Queen's annual Trooping the Colour celebrations.

What's On? Transformed into a beach for the Olympic Games, fans will flock there to watch Beach Volleyball.

Hyde Park

What's There? London's largest Royal Park has been open to the public since 1637 and remains a popular place to relax.

What's On? If you want to watch the Triathlon and the 10km Marathon Swimming, Hyde Park is the place to be.

Lord's Cricket Ground

What's There? Middlesex County Cricket Club play at Lord's, which has been a venue for first-class cricket since the late 19th Century.
What's On? Rather than cricket (which isn't an Olympic sport) this famous old ground will host the Archery events.

The Mall

What's There? A world-famous road that runs from Buckingham Palace to Trafalgar Square.
What's On? The Marathons, Race Walks and Cycling Road Races (except the Time Trial) will end on this iconic road.

North Greenwich Arena

What's There? Formerly known as the Millennium Dome, this fantastic indoor stadium is now famous for hosting music concerts.
What's On? This wonderful arena will be the perfect setting for Artistic and Trampoline Gymnastics, Basketball and Wheelchair Basketball.

The Royal Artillery Barracks

What's There? This historic building used to be home to thousands of soldiers and was the place where most of Britain's military weapons were made for over 200 years.
What's On? Fittingly the Barracks will host Shooting, Paralympic Shooting and Paralympic Archery during the Games.

Wembley Arena

What's There? Built for the Empire Games in 1934, this was originally a swimming pool but now it's famous for staging music concerts.
What's On? The world's greatest Badminton players will do battle inside the arena, as will competitors in Rhythmic Gymnastics.

Wembley Stadium

What's There? The impressive home of English football was rebuilt between 2003 and 2006 at a cost of £798 million.
What's On? No surprises here – several Olympic Football matches will take place at Wembley, including the men's and women's finals.

Wembley Stadium has more toilets than any other venue on the planet with 2,618.

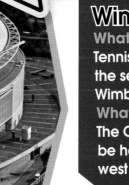

Wimbledon

What's There? The All England Lawn Tennis & Croquet Club has been the setting for the world-famous Wimbledon tournament since 1877.
What's On? No surprises here either! The Olympic tennis competitions will be held on the legendary south-west London grass courts.

Paralympic Judo

★ Star Turn

Name: Ben Quilter
Date Of Birth: 8 November 1981 (Brighton)
Event: Extra Light Weight (up to 60kg)
The Lowdown: Ben became Britain's first visually-impaired judo World Champion for 12 years when he triumphed at the 2010 event in Tokyo. He was also fifth at Beijing 2008.

Amazing Art

Judo is for blind, visually-impaired and deaf competitors. ParalympicsGB has won 13 medals so far and our best competitor was Simon Jackson, who won three gold and one bronze medal between Seoul 1988 and Athens 2004.

ParalympicsGB

How Does It Work?

Competitors lock, grip and grapple on a specially designed mat with different textured surfaces to denote the competition areas, aiming to score points during each five-minute match. They are divided up into different weight categories, from Extra Lightweight to Heavyweight.

Powerlifting

An incredible 10 Powerlifting world records were smashed at the Beijing 2008 Paralympic Games.

Pumped Up

Men's Powerlifting has been a Paralympic sport since Tokyo 1964, while women have been competing since Sydney 2000. Britain's star lifter is Emma Brown, who won gold at Sydney 2000 and Athens 2004 in her Up to 82.5kg category.

How Does It Work?

Lying on their backs on a weightlifting bench, competitors try to lift weights that get heavier with each round. The winner is the one who lifts the heaviest weight. There are 10 different weight categories for both men and women.

Paralympic Rowing

Power Stroke

Paralympic Rowing will make only its second appearance in 2012, but ParalympicsGB topped the medal table at Beijing 2008 with two golds from Tom Aggar and Helene Raynsford and bronzes from Vicki Hansford, Naomi Riches, Alastair McKean and James Morgan in the Mixed Coxed Four race.

★ Star Turn

Name: Tom Aggar
Date of Birth: 24 May 1984 (London)
Event: Single Sculls (ASM1x)
The Lowdown: Tom is the reigning Olympic and World Champion in the Single Scull class. He won gold at Beijing 2008 in only his second year of competitive rowing and was crowned World Champion in 2010 after winning the final by a massive 13 seconds.

How Does It Work?

London 2012 will have four rowing events – the Coxed Fours and Double Sculls (with mixed crews of men and women), plus Single Sculls events for men and women. The Coxed Four features rowers using one oar each, coached by a cox. In a scull, each rower uses two oars. All the races will be held over a 1000m course. Every boat is adapted with equipment such as special seats to match any competitors' level of disability.

Where and When
Eton Dorney, Friday 31 August
– Sunday 2 September

There will be 96 rowers competing for the medals at London 2012 – 48 men and 48 women.

41

Rowing

Oarsome Athletes

Great Britain's rowers were in world-beating form at the Beijing 2008 Games, winning two gold, two silver and two bronze medals to come top of the Rowing medals table. That performance followed their four-medal haul at Athens 2004. Team GB are looking for more glory at London 2012.

How Does It Work?

There are 14 Rowing events on the water at Eton Dorney in 2012. Rowers compete in boats of one, two, four or eight rowers. The smallest boats have solo rowers, who compete in the Single Sculls, while the biggest boats have eight rowers and a cox, who steers the boat and directs tactics during a race. Races are held head-to-head and the first boat over the finishing line is the winner. Heats (early knock-out races) show who the fastest crews are, who race in further rounds to reach the final. All events are held over a distance of 2000m.

'The Olympics happening in London is a once-in-a-lifetime opportunity.'

Greg Searle, gold medallist

Rowing is the only Olympic sport in which competitors cross the finishing line backwards.

Star Turn

Name: Zac Purchase and Mark Hunter
Date of Birth: 2 May 1986 (Cheltenham) and 1 July 1978 (London)
Event: Lightweight Double Sculls (2x)
The Lowdown: Zac and Mark struck gold at Beijing 2008 and lots of great results since then mean they will be looking for another gold in 2012.

Where and When
Eton Dorney, Saturday 28 July – Saturday 4 August

Numbers Game

There are two different ways of rowing – sculling and sweeping. Sculling involves each crew member rowing with two oars, one in each hand. Sweeping is rowing with a single oar, held in both hands.

Our most successful Olympic rower is Steve Redgrave, who won an incredible five gold medals in a row between 1984 and 2000.

Name: Katherine Grainger and Anna Watkins
Date of Birth: 12 November 1975 (Glasgow) and 13 February 1983 (Leek)
Event: Double Sculls (2x)
The Lowdown: Katherine won a silver medal at Beijing 2008 in the Quadruple Sculls, while Anna was a bronze medallist in the Double Sculls. The pair joined forces in 2010 and are looking for more success in 2012.

550

The number of rowers who will be competing on the lake at Eton Dorney.

The sport has featured at every single Olympic Games since its debut at Paris 1900.

Ones to Watch:

Steve Williams – Part of the crew that won gold at Beijing 2008 in the men's Fours (4-), Steve was also a champion at Athens 2004.

Stephen Rowbotham – Stephen made his Olympic debut at Beijing 2008, winning a bronze medal with Matt Wells in the Double Sculls (2x).

Number of lanes at Eton Dorney – eight for races and one 'return' lane for competitors.

9

70

Maximum weight in kilograms for a male rower in the Lightweight events.

TEAM GB and PARALYMPICSGB by Numbers

311
Number of athletes who represented Team GB at the Beijing 2008 Olympic Games.

5
Different Paralympic events that have been won by all-rounder Sarah Storey including races in both Swimming and Cycling.

104
Years since Team GB came first in the Olympic Games medals table.

22
Hours every week Rebecca Adlington spends in the swimming pool training for the Olympic Games.

4,926
Miles between Mo Farah's London home and his training camp in Oregon, USA.

41
Swimming medals won by ParalympicsGB in Beijing in 2008.

310
Millions of pounds from the National Lottery that has been spent supporting Team GB's Olympic and Paralympic athletes since 2006.

0
Number of Team GB Diving Olympic gold medals. Can Tom Daley be the first?

7
Meals a day eaten by Team GB's cyclists as they burn off thousands of calories riding their bikes.

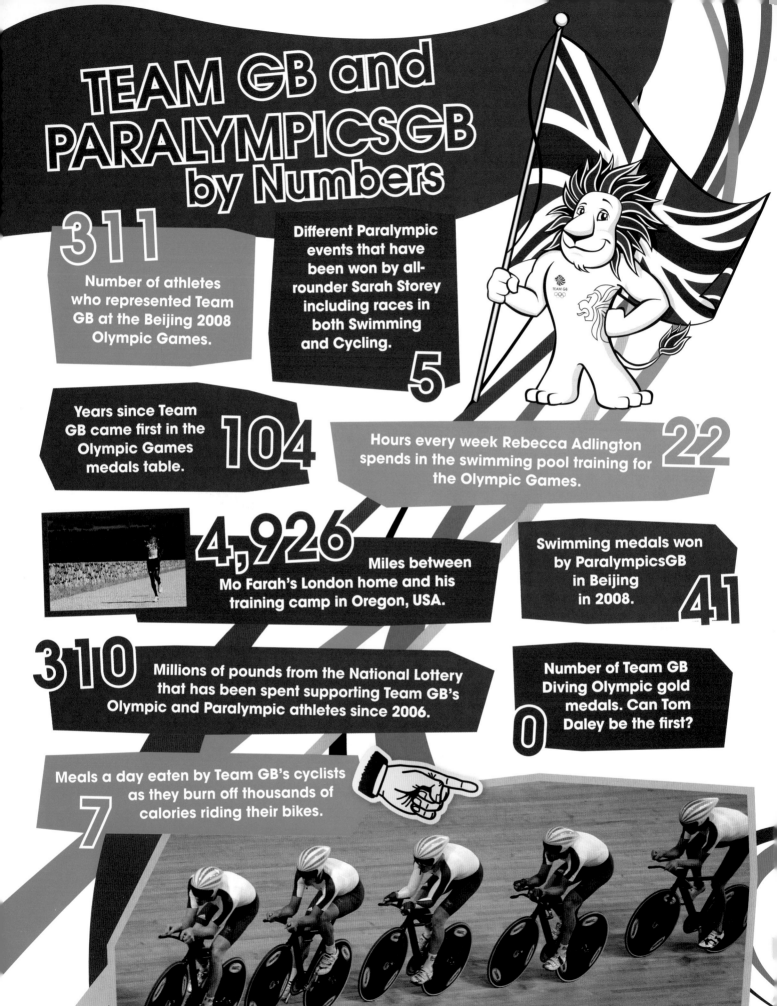

Standing in second place on the all-time Paralympic medal table with an impressive tally of 493 gold medals, ParalympicsGB has always been a force to be reckoned with. Here are some of our greatest Paralympic heroes.

ParalympicsGB

Mike Kenny (Paralympic Swimming)

Britain's most successful Paralympian of all-time collected a mind-boggling 16 gold medals from four fabulous Games between 1976 and 1988. He won titles in Backstroke, Breaststroke and Freestyle events. In his era, the Paralympic Games didn't receive the coverage it does today, making Kenny's achievements even more fantastic.

Tanni was born with the name Carys but her elder sister nicknamed her 'Tiny', pronounced it 'Tanni', and the name stuck.

Tanni Grey-Thompson (Paralympic Athletics)

Whether it was a marathon or a sprint, Tanni was always the woman to beat when it came to Paralympic Athletics, winning six London Marathons and an incredible 11 track gold medals in the 100m, 200m, 400m and 800m. Breaking an amazing 30 world records in a career that spanned 23 years, the Welsh legend is now coaching 2012 medal hopeful Jade Jones.

David can often be seen at Anfield supporting his beloved Liverpool FC, or at Bridgend Ravens cheering on his favourite rugby club.

David Roberts (Paralympic Swimming)

Four gold medals at the Beijing 2008 Games drew David level with fellow Welsh athlete Tanni Grey-Thompson on a total of 11 and the swimmer is desperate to add to his collection in London in 2012. The Freestyle specialist was given the honour of carrying the Union Jack flag at the closing ceremony four years ago and is regarded as one of ParalympicsGB's most inspirational performers.

Sailing

Riding the Waves

Sailing was one of Team GB's most successful events at Beijing 2008, with our men and women winning a magnificent four golds, a silver and a bronze medal in China.

Superb Team GB has topped the Sailing medals table at the last three Olympic Games.

How Does It Work?

There will be 14 days of action off the south coast of England during the London 2012 Games, featuring 380 of the world's finest sailors. Altogether, there are six events for men and four for women featuring different types of craft, from dinghies and keelboats to windsurfing boards. There are a total of 10 or 15 races: the winner of each race receives one point, the runner-up two points and so on. The individual sailor or team with the fewest points wins gold.

There are an estimated 2.5 million regular sailors around the world. Weymouth and Portland was the first of the London 2012 venues to be finished.

Where and When
Weymouth and Portland, Sunday 29 July – Saturday 11 August

Star Turn

Name: Ben Ainslie
Date of Birth: 5 February 1977 (Macclesfield)
Event: Finn class
The Lowdown: One of Team GB's most successful stars, Ben struck gold in the Laser class at the Sydney 2000 Games. He was also Olympic champion four years later when he triumphed in the Finn class at Athens 2004. Then he made it a hat-trick of gold medals at Beijing 2008 when he again won the Finn class.

46

Shooting

Magnificent Marksmen

A total of **390** competitors will descend on London to take part in the Shooting events. Team GB bagged a gold and a silver at the Sydney 2000 Games, but missed out on the medals at Beijing 2008.

Where and When
The Royal Artillery Barracks,
Saturday 28 July
– Monday 6 August

How Does It Work?

Olympic Shooting events fall into three types – Pistol, Rifle and Shotgun. In the Pistol and Rifle events, competitors aim at a ringed target from distances of 10m, 25m or 50m and must shoot from standing, kneeling or prone positions. Points are awarded for the closer they get to the middle of the target. In the Shotgun events, competitors take aim at moving clay targets launched into the air in front of them.

More than 275,000 clay targets will be blasted during the Shotgun events at London 2012.

Table Tennis

Fast and Furious

Table Tennis has been an Olympic sport since Seoul 1988 and is one of the Games' most action-packed events. China has dominated the event since its introduction, while Team GB is still waiting for its first medal.

Where and When
ExCeL, Saturday 28 July
– Wednesday 8 August

How Does It Work?

There are four medal events at London 2012 – the Singles and Team competitions, for both men and women. Singles (one player) matches are the best of seven games, with the first player to 11 points winning each game. Team matches feature four singles matches and one doubles (two player) match, each played over the best of five games. All four events are knockout competitions.

Paralympic Sailing

High Seas

ParalympicsGB has yet to win a Sailing medal since it became a full event at Sydney 2000, but hopes are high for 2012.

Where and When
Weymouth and Portland, Saturday 1 September – Thursday 6 September

How Does it Work?

Sailors compete in three mixed events – the Single-Person, Two-Person and Three-Person Keelboat competitions. The design of the boats provides stability on the water but otherwise they are very similar to the boats used in the Olympic Games.

★ Star Turn

Name: Alex Rickham
Date of Birth: 11 September 1981 (Jamaica)
Event: Two-Person Keelboat
The Lowdown: With team-mate Niki Birrell, Alex has won three World Championships and two World Cup golds in the Skud-18 Pairs event. He came fifth at Beijing 2008, and will be hoping for more at 2012.

Sitting Volleyball

Up and Over

Sitting Volleyball has been part of the Paralympic Games programme since Arnhem 1980 and other than the rule that states all players must be seated, is identical to volleyball.

During a game, players must always have a part of their body between their buttocks and their back on the floor.

How Does It Work?

The sport is contested between two teams of six on a 10 x 6m indoor court with a net 1.15m high for a men's game and 1.05m for a women's match. The aim of the game is to land the ball in the opponent's half and each side is allowed three touches to get the ball back over the net. Sets are won by the first team to reach 25 points and matches are the best of five sets.

Where and When
ExCeL, Thursday 30 August – Saturday 8 September

Paralympic Shooting

British Paralympic shooter Isabel Newstead won a remarkable 10 gold medals before her death in 2007.

On Target

A Paralympic event since the Arnhem 1980 Games, Shooting has proved a successful sport for Team GB over the years and British marksmen and women have won medals at every single Paralympic Games since.

How Does It Work?

Competitors take aim from a distance of 10, 25 or 50m in either a standing, kneeling or prone position. Points are won by hitting the target – 10 rings with the key one being the bullseye. Paralympic Shooting is open to athletes with any kind of disability. There are four different types of firearm: rifle, air rifle, pistol and air pistol.

Where and When
The Royal Artillery Barracks, Thursday 30 August – Thursday 6 September

Star Turn

Name: Matt Skelhon
Date of Birth: 30 October 1984 (Peterborough)
Event: 10m Air Rifle Prone (SH1 category)
The Lowdown: Matt hit the headlines with a sensational gold at the Beijing 2008 Paralympic Games in the 10m Air Rifle Prone – SH1 event and again in 2010 when he won the team competition in the same event at the World Cup in Turkey.

Paralympic Table Tennis

Where and When
ExCeL, Thursday 30 August – Saturday 8 September

How Does It Work?

Open to players in wheelchairs as well as those who can stand, a match is made up of the best of five 'games', with the first to 11 points winning a 'game'. There are singles and doubles competitons.

Table Matters

Paralympic Table Tennis first appeared at Rome 1960 and is now played in over 100 countries. Open to competitors with a range of disabilities, it is one of the fastest, most explosive sports. It is also one of the biggest sports at the Paralympic Games.

Venues Outside London

The London 2012 Games are not just being held in the capital of England. These 10 stunning venues around the UK will also be playing a huge part as hosts.

Brands Hatch

What's There? Kent's world-famous motor racing circuit has hosted 12 British Formula One Grand Prix and many other important races.

What's On? Paralympic Road Cycling will take centre stage on the circuit in races ranging from 30km to 120km in length.

The City of Coventry Stadium cost £113 million to build.

City of Coventry Stadium

What's There? Built in 2005, this all-seater ground is the home of Coventry City Football Club.

What's On? During the Games, 12 Olympic Football matches will take place here, including the women's bronze medal match.

Eton Dorney

What's There? A 2,200m long still-water lake in Buckinghamshire, owned by Eton College.

What's On? Team GB's and ParalympicsGB's Rowing teams will showcase their talents at this venue, which is also staging the Canoe Sprint.

Hadleigh Farm

What's There? A 700-acre working farm in Essex that features hilly woodland and beautiful grasslands.

What's On? Mountain Biking will transform this peaceful area during the course of the Olympic Games.

Hampden Park

What's There? Glasgow's revamped national football stadium hosts Scotland's international fixtures and major Scottish cup finals.

What's On? A total of eight men's and women's Olympic Football games will be held in front of Glasgow's passionate fans.

Lee Valley White Water Centre

What's There? Just over 30km north of the Olympic Park is this Hertfordshire centre featuring two stunning new Canoe Slalom courses.

What's On? The world's finest slalom canoeists will be racing down this arduous course as quickly and as accurately as they can.

Millennium Stadium

What's There? The home of the Wales' football and rugby national teams is a spectacular stadium, in Cardiff.

What's On? The very first event of the Olympic Games on 24 July will be a women's Football match in Cardiff and it will also host the men's bronze medal match.

The Millennium Stadium in Cardiff hosted six FA Cup Finals between 2001 and 2006.

St James' Park

What's There? Situated in the heart Newcastle, this football stadium is the home of Newcastle United.

What's On? Two quarter-final matches will be staged at this north-east venue, plus seven other matches.

Weymouth and Portland is located 120 miles south west of the Olympic Park.

Old Trafford

What's There? Manchester United's stadium is the Premier League's biggest ground, known as the 'Theatre of Dreams'.

What's On? Nine Football matches will take place at Old Trafford, including a semi-final in both the men's and women's tournaments.

Weymouth and Portland

What's There? The National Sailing Academy in Dorset has some of the best sailing conditions and facilities in the world.

What's On? Sailing and Paralympic Sailing will thrill crowds on the shore throughout the Games.

Lee Valley's Canoe Slalom course drops 5.5m from the high start line to the finish at the bottom.

Aquatics – Swimming

Pool Perfection

Swimming took place in a pool (rather than in the sea or a river) for the first time at London 1908 and is now one of the most popular events. At the last Olympic Games, Team GB won six medals – their best result since that first London Games.

Star Turn

Name: Rebecca Adlington
Date of Birth: 17 February 1989 (Mansfield)
Events: 400m Freestyle and 800m Freestyle
The Lowdown: Team GB's most successful swimmer for 100 years is hoping to follow up her amazing two gold medals at Beijing 2008 with more podium places in London. The star was awarded an OBE by the Queen in 2009.

Lake Legends

Hyde Park's historic Serpentine Lake is the venue for Swimming's 10km Marathon race. This two-hour gruelling swim is one of the toughest events at the Games as 50 swimmers try to be the first over the line. Team GB's Kerri-Anne Payne is our strongest hope for a medal.

At London 1908, the pool was a large outdoor tank in the White City Olympic Stadium.

Ones to Watch:

Liam Tancock – The world 50m Backstroke champion will also be a threat in the 100m.
Hannah Miley – A brilliant all-rounder, Hannah is a 400m Individual Medley star.
Ellen Gandy – The 200m Butterfly star is looking for Olympic success in 2012.

At the Paris 1900 Games, Underwater Swimming was an official event.

'I've never raced in front of a home crowd … It would be just an amazing day.'

Rebecca Adlington, double gold medallist

How Does It Work?

There are seven different types of race in the pool for men and women – Freestyle (usually done as front crawl), Breaststroke, Backstroke, Butterfly, Freestyle Relay, Individual Medley and Medley Relay. The Medley events combine all four of the strokes in the same race while Relays are done in teams of four. Races are held in lengths between 50m and 1,500m. Knock-out heats decide the eight finalists for each event and whoever wins the final takes gold. A 10km Marathon race will be held outdoors in Hyde Park's Serpentine lake.

After competing in just three Games so far, American swimmer Michael Phelps has won 14 gold medals – an Olympic record.

Where and When
POOL EVENTS: Aquatics Centre, Saturday 28 July – Saturday 4 August
10KM MARATHON: Hyde Park, Thursday 9 August – Friday 10 August

Paralympic Swimming

Watery Wonders

Swimming is the one of the biggest events at the Paralympic Games. At Beijing 2008, ParalympicsGB stars won 41 medals including 11 golds, a fantastic performance.

ParalympicsGB

Ones to Watch:

Liz Johnson – Won gold four years ago in the 100m Breaststroke and is aiming for a repeat at London 2012.
David Roberts – Legendary ParalympicsGB Freestyle star, who has amassed 11 Paralympic gold medals so far.
Fran Williamson – The reigning 50m Backstroke world champion is in great form.

How Does It Work?

The four main strokes – Freestyle (usually done as front crawl), Breaststroke, Backstroke and Butterfly all feature in Paralympic Swimming. Further events are the Individual Medley, Freestyle Relay and Medley Relay. Medley races are made up of the four main strokes while Relays are raced in teams of four. Swimmers are split into different categories depending on their disability. They are allowed to start each race inside or outside the pool, sitting, standing or on starting blocks. Races are swum from 50m to 400m and heats decide the eight finalists for each event. The first to the finish is the winner.

Star Turn

Name: Sam Hynd
Date of Birth: 3 July 1991 (Sutton)
Events: 400m Freestyle and 200m Individual Medley (S8 and SM8 categories)
The Lowdown: Sam won gold and bronze medals at Beijing 2008 – a stunning result at his first Paralympic Games. He has smashed world records along the way, too. He is one of ParalympicsGB's brightest hopes for London 2012.

South African Natalie Du Toit became the first Paralympic swimmer to qualify for the Beijing 2008 Olympic Games. She swam against non-disabled athletes in the 10km Marathon.

Visually impaired swimmers can have a guide at the end of the pool, who tells them when to turn.

Partially sighted swimmers must wear blackout goggles that block their vision when racing totally blind competitors, so that everyone is even.

★ Star Turn
Name: Ellie Simmonds
Date of Birth: 11 November 1994 (Walsall)
Events: 100m Freestyle and 400m Freestyle (S6 category)
The Lowdown: Ellie became an overnight sensation at Beijing 2008 after winning gold medals in the 100m and 400m Freestyle races at the age of just 13! Later that year she won the BBC Young Sports Personality of the Year award before being handed an MBE by the Queen in 2009, becoming the youngest person ever to receive the honour. Now 17, the Freestyle star is hoping for more success in front of her home fans.

108 world records were smashed by swimmers at the Beijing 2008 Paralympic Games.

Where and When
Aquatics Centre, Thursday 30 August – Saturday 8 September

'I didn't know I'd won the 100m until I looked up at the scoreboard. At first it was just total shock, then I was over the moon.'

Ellie Simmonds, on Beijing 2008

Aquatics – Diving

Pool Acrobatics

Fans will marvel at the bravery and skill of the world's best divers at London 2012 as they each strive to produce the perfect dive. This is an Olympic discipline which has featured in the Olympic Games for 108 years.

★ Star Turn

Name: Tom Daley
Date of Birth: 21 May 1994 (Plymouth)
Events: 10m Platform and Synchronised 10m Platform
The Lowdown: Tom won a world title in the 10m Platform event in 2009, only a year after he reached the Olympic final as a 14-year-old! His hopes are high for London 2012.

Where and When
Aquatics Centre, Sunday 29 July – Saturday 11 August

How Does It Work?

Dives take place in four events – the 3m Springboard, the 10m Platform and a Synchronised competition from 3m and 10m. Each diver is awarded a score out of 10 by a selection of eagle-eyed judges, who base their marks on the difficulty of the dive and the diver's technique. In the Synchronised event, two team-mates dive together in an attempt to produce a perfectly executed dive.

The first-ever diving competitions date back to the 18th century in Sweden and Germany.

Aquatics – Synchronised Swimming

Underwater Ballet

Contested as an Olympic discipline since 1984, Synchronised Swimming is all about impressing the judges with choreographed dance routines in the water.

Where and When
Aquatics Centre, Sunday 5 August – Friday 10 August

How Does It Work?

Swimmers in either pairs or teams of eight perform short routines to music and a panel of judges score them on style, difficulty and technique. This is one of just two Olympic events – the other being Rhythmic Gymnastics – that is women-only.

Tennis

Where and When
Wimbledon, Saturday 28 July
– Sunday 5 August

Charlotte Cooper was the first woman to win gold in an individual event when she won the Tennis Singles at Paris 1900.

Wimbledon Wonders

Great Britain won all six gold medals the last time Olympic Tennis was held on the grass courts of the famous Wimbledon venue in 1908. Superstar Andy Murray is Team GB's brightest hope for London 2012.

How Does It Work?

There are three events in Tennis – Singles (one player) and Doubles (two players) for men and women, plus Mixed Doubles (where teams of men and women play together). Matches are played over the best of three sets in the men's and women's Singles and Doubles, except for the showpiece men's Singles final, which is the best of five sets. Mixed Doubles contests are decided by a tie-break if the teams are level at one set all.

★ Star Turn

Name: Aaron Cook
Date of Birth: 2 January 1991 (Dorchester)
Event: Under 80kg
The Lowdown: Aaron just missed out on a bronze medal for Team GB at the Beijing 2008 Games but has since become European champion in his weight category.

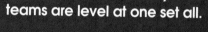

Taekwondo

Martial Arts Magic

This combat sport only made its debut as a full Olympic event at Sydney 2000 and has been dominated ever since by the Republic of Korea and China.

Where and When
ExCeL, Wednesday 8 August
– Saturday 11 August

How Does It Work?

The object is to land punches and kicks on an opponent in three two-minute rounds. Competitors have their heads and torsos protected by coloured padding. A successful punch or kick to the torso is worth one point, a spinning kick wins two points and four points are awarded if an athlete can kick their opponent's head with a spinning kick. The competitor with the most points wins.

099

Triathlon

Where and When
Hyde Park, Saturday 4 August
and Tuesday 7 August

Ultimate Athletes

This relatively new Olympic sport took place for the first time at the Sydney 2000 Games and Team GB is looking to win its first medal at 2012 through our brightest hope, Alistair Brownlee.

How Does It Work?

Swimming, cycling and running are the three ingredients that make up a Triathlon, all following on non-stop. The athletes begin with a 1500m swim in Hyde Park's Serpentine Lake before grabbing their bikes for a 40km cycle race on the streets of London, then completing a 10km run back in Hyde Park. The first over the line wins.

★ Star Turn

Name: Alistair Brownlee
Date of Birth: 23 April 1988 (Dewsbury)
The Lowdown:
Having won the World Triathlon Championships in 2009 and 2011, Alistair is one of the favourites to land gold for Team GB in London. His younger brother Jonathan is one of his biggest rivals.

Volleyball

A Smashing Sport

Since its debut at Tokyo 1964 this fast and exciting sport has been one of the most popular at the Games. Beach Volleyball was added at Atlanta 1996 and both versions are bound to get everyone's pulse racing.

Some players can hit a volleyball so hard that it reaches a speed of 80mph.

Where and When
VOLLEYBALL: Earls Court,
Saturday 28 July
– Sunday 12 August

BEACH VOLLEYBALL: Horse Guards
Parade, Saturday 28 July –
Thursday 9 August

How Does It Work?

Six players make up a Volleyball team. Each side is allowed three touches of the ball before it has to cross the net and the aim is for the ball to hit the ground inside the opposition's area, which scores one point. The first to reach 25 points (or 15 points in the fifth set) wins a set and the first to win three sets takes the match. Beach Volleyball is played by two players per team. The court is outdoors and is covered in sand. Matches are the best of three sets, with 21 points (15 points in the third set) needed to win a set.

How Does It Work?

Two seven-a-side teams line up against each other in the water over four eight-minute periods. The object of the game is to throw the ball into the opposing team's net. Each team only has 30 seconds to score a goal and all players (except the goalkeepers) must only use one hand to catch or throw the ball. If they fail to score within 30 seconds, possession is handed to the other side.

Where and When
Water Polo Arena, Sunday 29 July
– Sunday 12 August

Aquatics –
Water Polo

Back in the Pool

Team GB won four of the first five Olympic Water Polo competitions but haven't competed in the event for 56 years. The home team will be looking to cause an upset in front of their fans.

⭐ ## Star Turn

Name: Zoe Smith
Date of Birth: 26 April 1994 (Greenwich)
Event: 58kg
The Lowdown: Zoe became the first English woman to win a Commonwealth Games medal in Weightlifting when landing bronze in 2010.

Weightlifters cover their hands in chalk before each lift to help them get a better grip on the bar.

Weightlifting

Raising the Bar

Weightlifting is a test of strength and some athletes can lift more than three times their own body weight! Competitors are divided up according to body weight, creating 15 gold medal events in this famous Olympic sport.

How Does It Work?

Men and women take part and complete two types of lift – the 'snatch' (where the bar is lifted from the floor to above the head in one movement) and a 'clean and jerk' (where the bar is brought up to rest on the shoulders first before being raised above the head). Each athlete has three attempts to lift each weight. Judges decide whether or not a lift has been successful.

Where and When
ExCeL, Saturday 28 July
– Tuesday 7 August

59

Wheelchair Basketball

ParalympicsGB

⭐ Star Turn
Name: Helen Freeman
Date of Birth: 23 November 1989 (Watford)
The Lowdown: Helen studies at university in America but travels back to the UK to represent ParalympicsGB on court and is often one of the team's highest point-scorers.

Court Rulers

After doing well at the recent European Championships, the ParalympicsGB squad will have high hopes of success on home soil. At Beijing 2008, the men's team won bronze.

How Does It Work?
The players in this 5-a-side game try to get the ball through a hoop. They get two points for a close-range 'basket' and three for a long-range one. Players must either pass or bounce the ball after every two pushes of their wheels. To ensure fairness, each player is given a points value based on their disability, ranging from 1 (highest) to 4.5 (lowest). The points total of the five players on court can't exceed 14 points.

Where and When
North Greenwich Arena and White Hall, Thursday 30 August – Saturday 8 September

Wheelchair Fencing

Swashbuckling Stars
Wheelchair Fencing has been an international sport since 1953. China is the dominant force at the moment.

Where and When
ExCeL, Tuesday 4 September – Saturday 8 September

The tip of each sword has a button that gets pressed and scores a point when a fencer hits their opponent cleanly.

How Does It Work?
There are three competitions – Epée, Foil and Sabre. The competitor with the shortest arm decides on the distance between wheelchairs, which are then strapped to the floor so they can't move. In the Epée, points are scored by hitting your rival anywhere above the waist with the tip of the sword. In the Foil, you may only aim for the opponent's body, while in the Sabre you can use the edge of the sword. There is also a Team event. Special masks and body armour protect the fencers.

Wheelchair Rugby

Fast and Tough

Wheelchair Rugby became a full medal sport at the Sydney 2000 Paralympic Games and Britain has qualified for every Games since. The team came fourth at Beijing 2008 after narrowly losing to eventual champions USA in the semi-finals.

Wheelchair Rugby's chairs are specially designed to withstand all the sport's collisions and can cost up to £5,000 each.

Where and When
White Hall, Wednesday 5 September – Sunday 9 September

How Does It Work?

Although it's called Wheelchair Rugby, the sport is more like a full-contact version of Wheelchair Basketball. It's a 4-a-side sport with eight substitutes and the aim is to charge over your opponent's goal line with the ball. Players with the ball must bounce it or pass within 10 seconds.

Serving Up a Treat

Wheelchair Tennis was added to the Paralympic Games schedule at Barcelona 1992 and to date Great Britain has won four medals. Legend Peter Norfolk has played a part in all four.

Wheelchair Tennis

How Does It Work?

Wheelchair Tennis is very similar to its Olympic counterpart. The big difference is that the ball is allowed to bounce twice in Wheelchair Tennis to give competitors more time to reach it.

Star Turn

Name: Peter Norfolk
Date of Birth: 13 December 1960 (London)
Event: Doubles – Quad
The Lowdown: A big star, Peter won ParalympicsGB's first-ever gold in the sport when he triumphed at Athens 2004. His Paralympic Games record is amazing, having won gold and silver in the Singles and Doubles at Athens 2004, then gold and bronze at Beijing 2008. He will be hoping to win a third gold at London 2012.

Where and When
Eton Manor, Saturday 1 September – Saturday 8 September

Wrestling

Test of Strength

One of the oldest Olympic sports (dating back to the ancient Games), Wrestling has two disciplines. The first, Greco-Roman, has been an Olympic discipline since the Athens 1896 Games. The second, Freestyle, was introduced at the St Louis 1904 Games. Team GB has gone more than 100 years without a Wrestling medal but hopes are high for London 2012.

Team GB has never won a Greco-Roman medal but has claimed three gold, four silver and 10 bronze medals in Freestyle.

How Does It Work?

Taking place on a circular mat, wrestlers aim to pin down their opponents or throw them to the ground.

In Greco-Roman, athletes are only allowed to use their arms and upper bodies to attempt moves and holds. In Freestyle, competitors may use any part of their bodies. Matches last for a maximum of three periods of two minutes, with a 30-second break in between periods. A contest can finish early if a wrestler wins the first two periods or pins down his opponent.

Men and women take part in Freestyle, but Greco-Roman is men-only. Competitors are grouped by their body weight.

Where and When
ExCeL, Sunday 5 – Sunday 12 August

Star Turn

Name: Leon Rattigan
Date of Birth: 4 October 1987 (Bristol)
Event: Freestyle
The Lowdown: Britain has not won an Olympic Wrestling medal since London 1908, but after Leon claimed bronze at the 2010 Commonwealth Games, hopes are high that Team GB might win one.

344 men and women will descend on ExCeL in 2012 to grapple their way to glory.